Anthony Burgess

*An Enumerative Bibliography
With Selected Annotations*

By
Paul Boytinck

Norwood Editions / 1974

Limited to 200 Copies

INTRODUCTION

Anthony Burgess has delighted the world with his fiction, reviews and feuilletons. This bibliography is intended as a preliminary guide to his work for students and librarians. It lists, for example, nearly 300 book reviews of his major works, and cites 30 reviews of *A Clockwork Orange,* of which 11 are devoted to the book and 19 to the film.

Burgess is a prolific writer who often writes for old-fashioned Balzacian motives. His enviable flogging of paper in the best Grub Street tradition, and the demands of trans-Atlantic publication, have given his work some oddities.

First, there is the question of pseudonyms. John Anthony Burgess Wilson is his real name. "Anthony Burgess" was adopted for the three novels set in the East, apparently to obviate Colonial Office disapproval of a writer shackled to some anti-colonial attitudes. The name stuck, and it is the name under which he is generally known. However, in 1959 Burgess wrote five novels in one year. Use of still another pseudonym was considered expedient to head off reviewers' envious or foolishly querulous complaints of over-production. Burgess therefore chose the name Joseph Kell to grace *One Hand Clapping* and *Inside Mr. Enderby.*

Second there is the librarian's familiar but thorny problem of different titles for the same work. *The Long Day Wanes* is the American title for the *Malayan Trilogy.* Both titles include the same three novels: *Time for a Tiger* (1956), *Enemy in the Blanket* (1958) and *Beds in the East* (1959). The plain, unadorned *Enderby* includes both *Inside Mr. Enderby* and the continuation of that *borborygmic* picaro's adventures in *Enderby Outside.* Finally, *Here Comes Everybody* (British title) has been issued in the United States as *Re Joyce.*

Third, the British edition of *A Clockwork Orange* includes a final penitential chapter excluded from the

i

American edition. In the last chapter of the British edition, Alex meets one of his newly married former "droogs" and discovers, if not agonbite of inwit, at least the small, confortable stirrings of dissatisfaction with his past life of frothy ultraviolence and mechanical machismo. He sighs, in fact, for an agreeable domesticity, and regards his former acts as so many juvenalia. The American publishers lopped off that chapter and decided to take leave of an Alex unregenerate and unbowed. The film, of course, does the same.

Some important but random remarks. Those readers interested in the chronological order of Burgess' books should consult the chronological table at the end of this bibliography. Many of Burgess' articles listed on pp. 11-24 of this work under the heading entitled "Articles, Essays, Reviews, Etc." are also included in *Urgent Copy*, a collection of Burgess' critical pieces. Printer's ink has been sacrificed in favor of the fullest possible form of citation. This remark holds true of the last section of the bibliography which gives reviews of Burgess' books. Not all of these or other citations were personally examined. Any notice of errors or omissions will be gratefully acknowledged, and they will help to shore up a planned second edition of this work when Burgess has had time to add to the world's memorable stock of philosophical conundrums, worldly glosses, kindly judgments, liberating verbal experiments — and when he has been given a decently grateful interval to exeleutherostomize.

PAUL BOYTINCK
ELLEN CLARKE BERTRAND LIBRARY
LEWISBURG, PA.

ACKNOWLEDGMENTS

The annotations found in this work derive from several sources. Some are reprinted from *The New York Times Index*. Others, the great majority, are taken verbatim from *Abstracts of English Studies* (cited as AES) and *Historical Abstracts. A: Modern History*. The unsigned annotations are generally my own or freely adapted from other sources. The publishers of these indexes and abstracts have my grateful thanks for permission to reprint the text of these annotations. My thanks are also due to the librarians of Bucknell University, Lewisburg, Pa., who generously brought many citations to my attention; to the University itself for a travel grant to State College; and to my friend, Prudencio de Pereda, who helped me immeasurably in many ways.

CONTENTS

Fiction and Non-Fiction

Age of the Grand Tour. 1967.
London: Elek, 1967.

Beds in the East. 1959.
London: Heinemann, 1959.
London: Heinemann, 1968.

Clockword Condition. May 1973.
New York: Knopf, forthcoming.

Clockwork Orange. 1962.
London: Heinemann, 1962.
New York: Norton, 1963. pap.
New York: Modern Library, 1968.
New York: Ballantine, 1971 (c1963).

Coaching Days of England. 1966.
London: Elek, 1966.

Devil of a State. 1961.
London: Heinemann, 1961.
New York: Norton, 1962.
New York: Ballantine. pap.

Doctor is Sick. 1960.
London: Heinemann, 1960.
New York: Norton, 1966.
New York: Ballantine, 1966. pap.

Enderby. 1968.
New York: Norton, 1968.
New York: Ballantine, 1969. pap.

Enderby Outside. 1968.
London: Heinemann, 1968.
Harmondsworth: Penguin. 1971. pap.

Enemy in the Blanket. 1958.
    London: Heinemann, 1958.
    London: Heinemann, 1968.

English Literature; A Survey for Students.
    London: Longmans, 1958.

Eve of Saint Venus. 1964.
    London: Sidgwick and Jackson, 1964.
    Rexdale, Ont.: Ambassador Books (1964?)
    New York: Norton, 1970.
    New York Ballantine, 1971. pap.

Here Comes Everybody. 1965.
    London: Faber, 1965.
    London: Faber, 1969. pap.

Honey for the Bears. 1963.
    London: Heinemann, 1963.
    New York: Norton, 1964.
    London: Pan Books, 1965. pap.

Inside Mr. Enderby. 1963.
    London: Heinemann, 1963.
    Harmondsworth: Penguin, 1966.

Language Made Plain. 1964.
    London: English Universities Press, 1964.
    New York: Crowell, 1965.
    New York: Crowell, 1969.
    New York: Apollo Editions, 1969. pap.

The Long Day Wanes. 1965.
    New York: Norton, 1965.
    New York: Ballantine, 1966. pap.

MF. 1971.
    London: Cape, 1971.
    New York: Knopf, 1971.
    New York: Ballantine, 1972. pap.

Malayan Trilogy. 1964.
    London: Pan Books, 1964.

Nothing Like the Sun. 1964.
> London: Heinemann, 1964.
> Don Mills, Ontario: Collins (1964).
> New York: Norton, 1964.
> Harmondsworth: Penguin, 1966.

Novel Now. 1967.
> London: Faber and Faber, 1967.
> New York: Norton, 1967.
> New York: Pegasus, 1970.
> London: Faber and Faber, 1971. New ed.

Novel Today.
> London: British Council, 1963
> London?) Folcroft Library Editions, 1971.

One Hand Clapping. 1961.
> London: Davies, 1961.
> New York: Knopf, 1972.
> New York: Ballantine, 1973.

Re Joyce. 1964.
> New York: Ballantine, 1965. pap.
> New York: Norton, 1965.
> New York: Norton, 1968.
> Magnolia, Mass.: Peter Smith.

Right to an Answer. 1960.
> London: Heinemann, 1960.
> New York: Norton, 1961.

Shakespeare. 1970.
> London: Cape, 1970.
> New York: Knopf, 1970.

Time for a Tiger. 1956.
> London: Heinemann, 1956.
> London: Heinemann, 1968.

Tremor of Intent. 1966.
      London: Heinemann, 1966.
      New York: Norton, 1966.
      New York: Ballantine, 1972 (c1966) pap.

Urgent Copy. 1968.
      London: Cape, 1968.
      New York: Norton, 1969.

Vision of Battlements. 1965.
      London: Sidgwick and Jackson, 1965.
      New York: Norton, 1966.

Wanting Seed. 1962.
      London: Heinemann, 1962.
      New York: Ballantine, 1962.
      New York: Norton, 1963.
      New York: Ballantine, 1970. pap.

The Worm and the Ring. 1961.
      London: Heinemann, 1961.
      London: Heinemann, 1970. Rev. ed.

Stories

"Muse" *Hudson Review,* v. 21 (Spring 1968) 109-26.

"Somebody's Got to Pay the Rent" *Partisan Review,*
v. 35 (Winter 1968) 67-74.

Other Works Edited, Adapted, Translated, Etc.

Collier, John. *The John Collier Reader.*
  Introduction by Anthony Burgess. New York: Knopf, 1972.

Defoe, Daniel. *Journal of the Plague Year.*
  Edited by Anthony Burgess and Christopher Bristow, with an
  introduction by Anthony Burgess. Harmondsworth: Penguin,
  1966.

Joyce, James. *A Shorter Finnegan's Wake.*
  London: Faber, 1966. pap.
  Seattle: University of Washington Press, 1966.
  Toronto: Macmillan, 1966.
  New York: Viking, 1967.
  New York: Viking, 1968.
  Toronto: Macmillan (1968) pap.

Kubrick, Stanley. *A Clockwork Orange.*
  New York: Abelard-Schuman, 1971.

Mozart, Johann Wolfgang Chrysostom Amadeus.
Don Giovanni. Idomeneo.
  Introduction by Anthony Burgess. London: Cassell, 1971.

  New York: Universe Books, 1971.

Rostand, Edmund. *Cyrano de Bergerac.*
  Translated and adapted for the Modern Stage by Anthony
  Burgess. New York: Knopf, 1971.

Saint-Pierre, Michel de. *The New Aristocrats.*
  Translated by Anthony and Llewela Burgess. London: Gol-
  lancz, 1962.

Sophocles. *Oedipus the King.*
Translated and adapted by Anthony Burgess. With comments
by Anthony Burgess, Michael Langham, and Stanley Silver-
man. Minneapolis: University of Minnesota Press in Associa-
tion with the Guthrie Theater, 1972.

Translations Into
Foreign Languages

Age of the Grand Tour.

La Bella Europa (Italian). Trans., Francisco Mei. Roma: Editalia, 1970.

Le Grand Siecle de Voyage. Paris: Michel, 1968.

A Clockwork Orange.

Un' Arancia a Orologeria (Italian). Trans., Floriana Bossi. Torino: Einaudi, 1969.

Orange Mecanique. Paris: Laffont, 1972.

The Doctor is Sick.

Der Doktor ist Ubergeschnappt (German). Trans., Inge Wiskott. Tubingen: Erdmann, 1968.

Der Doktor ist Ubergeschnappt. Eine Groteske Geschichte aus Londons Unterwelt (German). Trans., Inge Wiskott. Reinbek bei Hamburg: Rowohlt, 1970.

Here Comes Everybody.

Ein Mann in Dublin Namens Joyce (German). Trans., Gisela und Manfred Triesch. Bad Homburg: Gehlen, 1968.

Honey for the Bears.

Honig fur die Baren (German). Trans., Dorothea Gotfart. Tubingen: Erdmann, 1967.

Honig fur die Baren (German). Trans., Dorothea Gotfart. Reinbek bei Hamburg: Rowohlt, 1971.

Nothing Like the Sun.

Intet Ar Som Solen. En Gerattelse on Shakespeares Kaleksliv. (Swedish). Trans., Ake Oilmarks. Stockholm: Bonnier, 1964.   ,

Novel Now.

Gendai Shosetsu To Wa Naniki. (Japanese). Trans., Makawa Yuichi. Tokyo: Takeuchi Shoten, 1970.

Tremor of Intent.

Martyrernes Blod (Danish). Trans., Harry Mortensen. Copenhagen: Spektrum, 1969.

Un Agent Qui Vous Veut du Bien (French). Trans., Michel Deutsch. Paris: Denoel, 1969.

The Wanting Seed.

Du Skal Aede din Naeste (Danish). Trans., Michael Tjen. Copenhagen: Schonborg, 1963.

Articles, Essays, Reviews, Etc.

"Anatomy of Melancholy," *Horizon*, v. 12 *(Autumn 1970) 48-53.*

"Anthony Burgess Meets New York," *New York Times Magazine*, October 29, 1972, p. 28.

> Also a letter, *New York Times Magazine*, November 19, 1972, p.34.

"Bagehot on Books," *Spectator*, v. 216, no. 7176 (January 7, 1966) 15.

> Review article of *The Collected Works of Walter Bagehot*, vols. I and II. Bagehot's literary criticism has been suspect for two reasons: the obvious fact that literature is merely one of his interests; and the evidence that he enjoyed reading books. His approach to an author is human; he sees the works as an emanation of personality; and he judges the disclosed personality with charity. — AES, v. 9, no. 8 (October 1966) 525. No. 2732.

"Bless thee, Bottom . . ." *Times Literary Supplement*, September 18, 1970, p. 1024-5.

"Boo," *New York Times Book Review*, VII, Part II (February 11, 1973) 2.

> An omnibus review of current Gothic and supernatural fiction available in paper-back. He is respectful of Tom Tryon's *The Other* and Peter Blatty's *The Exorcist*, but has exuberant fun with what he calls "femfic" — the cliche-ridden Gothic fiction written mainly by women for women.

"The Book is not for Reading," *New York Times Book Review*, December 4, 1966, p. 1.

An account of Burgess' reading habits; laments inability to tackle Jane Austen; his preferred fiction has "a strong male thrust, an almost pedantic allusiveness, and a brutal intellectual content."

"Brothers Grimm and their Famous Law for Linguists," *Horizon*, v. 10 (Winter 1968) 66-72.

"The Canterbury Tales," *Horizon*, v. 13, no. 2 (Spring 1971) 44-59.
   With drawings by Z. Blum

"Cast a Cold Eye," *Spectator*, v. 214, no. 7125 (January 15, 1965) 73.
   Review article of Edward Engelberg's *The Vast Design — Patterns in W. B. Yeats' Aesthetic*; Peter Ure's *Yeats*; and *W. B. Yeats — Selected Criticism*, edited by A. Norman Jeffares. Yeats' content resolves into the common stock of all poets: the opposition of the moving to the static, the agony of transcience; the need to build something on which to rejoice. His achievement was not a "system" but an "astonishing rhetoric or grandiloquence." His tone fits well the "oratorical needs" of a word-conscious emergent nation. — AES, v.8, no.8 (October 1965) 461. No.2392.

"Clockwork Marmalade," *Listener*, v. 87, no 2238 (February 17, 1972) (197)-199.
   Not an adverse judgment on the filmed version of *A Clockwork Orange* but an invaluable gloss on both book and film. He explains the origin of themes; explains choice of title and the book's neologistic language (called "nadsat" — from the Russian suffix for "teen," e.g., fifteen is "pyatnadsat"); clarifies issues; defends himself against detractors.

"The Comedy of Ultimate Truths," *Spectator*, v. 216, no. 7190 (April 15, 1966) 462.
   If Evelyn Waugh is to be remembered as a comic novelist, that implies no relegation to a secondary status. Comedy with

him was not merely entertainment: it was a medium for the expression for ultimate truths, some of them very bitter. Too many critics who have condemned alleged evidences of snobbery in his writings have missed something deeper even than the patrician pose that was inseparable from his comic technique: they missed the Shakespearean hunger for order and stability. — AES, v. 10, no. 2 (February 1967) 114. no.650.

"The Corruption of the Exotic," *Listener*, v. 70, no. 1800 (September 26, 1963) 465-467.

"Culture as a Hot Meal," *Spectator, v. 225, nos. 7410-11 (July 11, 1970) 13-14.*
> Review of *The Raw and the Cooked,* by Claude Levi-Straus.

"Daltonian Prejudice," *Guardian*, November 16, 1966, p. 20.

"Dear Mr. Shame's Voice," *Spectator*, v. 213, no. 7118 (November 27, 1964) 731-32.
> Review article of *Joyce's Portrait': Criticisms and Critiques,* edited by Thomas Connolly; Robert F. Ryf's *A New Approach to Joyce;* A Walton Litz's *The Art of James Joyce;* and Helmut Bonheim's *Joyce's Benefictions.* These four books may be of value to the British students of *Finnegan's Wake* — "all six of us" — but they confirm the belief that the time has come for Joyce to be "released from the Babylonish captivity of the Professors" and presented to the "ordinary decent prople who love books" as one of the great comic writers of all time." — AES, v.8, no.8 (October 1965) 460-61. no.2390.

"Democracy of Prejudice," *Encounter*, v.29 (August 1967) 71-5.

"Dickens Loud and Clear," *Spectator*, v.217, no. 7226 (December 23, 1966) 817.
> Review article of *Oliver Twist; the Clarendon Dickens,* edited by Kathleen Tillotson. It is too often forgotten that Dickens'

real predecessors are the Jacobean "humour" satirists. Like theirs, Dickens' achievement was to create serious literary art out of pop material.—AES, v.10, no.8 (October 1967) 538. no.2892.

"Did Shakespeare Mean That, or Is It a Printer's Error," *Chicago Tribune*, January 12, 1969, p.5.

"Don't Cook Mother Goose," *New York Times Book Review*, November 5, 1967, p. 1.

"Dr. Rowse meets Dr. Faustus," *Nation*, v. 200 (February 1, 1965) 115.
> Review of *Christopher Marlow*, by Alfred Leslie Rowse.

"Electric Grape," *American Scholar*, v. 35 (Autumn 1966) 719-20.

"Enemy of Twilight," *Spectator*, v. 217, no. 7204 (July 22, 1966) 124.
> Review article of J. M. Synge's *Collected Works, v.2; Prose*. Edited by Alan Price. The first volume of the collected works, Synge's verse, his translations, and varied fragments, confirmed the view that Synge was a minor poet. This volume gives us the raw material of the plays. And it reveals a master of English prose. — AES, v.10, no.2 (February 1967) 116. no.657.

"English as an America," *Encounter*, v.28 (February 1967) 67-71.

"Europe's Day of the Dead," *Spectator*, v.218, no. 7230 (January 20, 1967) 74.
> Review article of Malcolm Lowry's *Under the Volcano*. Lowry's hero, Geoffrey Firmin, is neither a Prufrock nor a Hamlet but a Promethean rebel ("perhaps the last exemplar of Liberal

Man") who is an exact symbol of the Europe of 1938-1939
—AES, v.10, no.8 (October 1967) 538. no.2893.

"Fed Up to Here; *New York Times* Book Review,
October 20, 1968, p.66-7.
> An Open Letter to the *New York Times*. Holds that far too
> many cook-books are being published; ridicules exotic foods
> featured in most cook-books.

"From A to ZZZ," *New York Times Book Review*
September 21, 1969, p. 2.
> Reviews merits of some American dictionaries.

"Future of Anglo-American," *Harper*, v. 236 (February 1968) 53-6.

"Genesis and Headache." In *Afterwords; Novelists
on Their Novels*, ed. by Thomas McCormack, p. 29-
47. New York: Harper, 1968.
> Describes the genesis of his novel *Nothing Like the Sun*.

"Gibraltar," *Holiday*, v.41 (February 1967) 70-1

"A Good Man Destroyed — Hilariously," *Life*, v.64
(March 15, 1970) 8.
> Review of Mordecai Richler's *Cocksure*.

"A Good Read," *New York Times Book Review*, June
15, 1969, p.2.
> Comments on lack in much current literature of books that are
> "good reads" — i.e., books that are meant to be read in
> spare time and have a general uplift; humorously suggests
> modern-day criticism will replace such "reads."

"Graves and Omar," *Encounter*, v.30 (January
1968) 77-8.

"The Great American Visionary," *Spectator*, v.216, no.7187 (March 25, 1966) 365.

A review of Walt Whitman's *Leaves of Grass*, edited by Harold W. Blodgett and Sculley Bradley. Whitman's verse-technique is still of interest to the prosodist. His basic rhythm is an epic one — the Virgilian dactyl-spondee — and his line often Hexametric. But, flouting classical procedure in refusing to allow any spill-over from line to line, he invokes a tradition older than Virgil — that of Hebrew poetry. As one of the 19th century innovators, Whitman can be ranked with Hopkins. — AES, v.10, no.2 (February 1967) 114, no.647.

"Great Mogul Beethoven: Genius Got in the Way," *Vogue*, v.155 (March 15, 1970) 132-3.

"Great Vowel Shift and All That," *Encounter*, v. 26 (May 1966) 70-3.

Linguistic knowledge, such as shown in Mario Pei's *The Story of Language*, will not help literature, but it will remove many misconceptions about the nature of language. — AES, v.10, no.2 (February 1967) 81. no.455.

"He Wrote Good," *Spectator*, v.217, no.7202 (July 8, 1966) 47.

Review article of A. E. Hotchner's *Papa Hemingway*. Both D. H. Lawrence and Hemingway revolted against the products of the highly refined intellect; the subject matter of both was instinctual, or natural, man. But Lawrence's prose was stuck in the pre-war age of rhetoric. Hemingway's achievement was to create a style exactly fitted for the exclusion of the cerebral. — AES, v.10, no. 2 (February 1967) 115. no.655.

"The Human Russians," *The Listener*, v.56 (December 28, 1961) 1106-8.

Reprinted in *Science Digest*, v.51 (May 1962) 33-37.

16

"I Love England But I Will No Longer Live There,"
New York Times Magazine, November 3, 1968,
p.39.

> Deplores current social scene in Great Britain; interview with
> A. Lewis — says he loves England, but prefers to live else-
> where rather than let all his earnings as writer "all go to the
> tax man" in service of a welfare state which has made Eng-
> land's prosperity "milk and water" — says that as Conserva-
> tive with Catholic background he never had any expectations
> from Socialism.

"Is America Falling Apart?" *New York Times Magazine,* November 7, 1971, p.99-104.

"Is Shakespeare Relevant?" *New York Times,* December 11, 1970, p. 47, column 4.

"Joyce Can't Really Be Imitated," *Books and Book-
men,* v.15 (July 1970) 8-9.

"Joyce Cary's Heroic Journey Up," *Life,* v.65 (October 25, 1968) 15.

"Joyce Industry in the United States," *Atlas,* v.10
(July 1965) 51-3.

> Reprint of "Dear Mr. Shame's Voice," first published in the
> *Spectator.*

"Language as Movement," *Encounter,* v.34 (January
1970) 64-7.

"Language, Myth and Mr. Updike," *Commonweal,*
v.83 (February 11, 1966) 557-9.

"Letter from England," *American Scholar,* v.36
(Spring 1967) 261-5.

"Letter from England," *Hudson Review,* v. 19 (Autumn 1966) 455-60.

"Letter from England," *Hudson Review*, v. 20 (Autumn 1967) 454-8.

"Letter from Europe," *American Scholar*, v. 38 (Spring-Autumn 1969) 297-9, 684-6.

"Letter from Europe," *American Scholar*, v. 39 (Summer 1970) 502-4.

"Letter from Europe," *American Scholar*, v. 40 (Winter 1970) 119-122.

"Letter from Europe," *American Scholar*, v. 40 (Summer 1971) 514-20.

"Letter from Europe," *American Scholar*, v. 41 (Summer 1972) 425-8.

"Letter from Europe," *American Scholar*, v. 41 (Winter 1971-72) 139-42.

"Letter from Europe," *American Scholar*, v. 42, no. 1 (Winter 1972-3) 135-8.

"London Letter," *American Scholar*, v. 36 (Autumn 1967) 636-8.

"London Letter," *American Scholar*, v. 37 (Spring 1968) 312-5.

"London Letter," *American Scholar*, v. 37 (Autumn 1968) 647-9.

"London Letter," *Hudson Review*, v. 19 (Autumn 1966) 455-60.

"London Letter," *Hudson Review*, v. 20 (Spring 1967) 99-104.

"Making de White Boss Frown," *Encounter*, v. 27 (July 1968) 54-8.
> Harriet Beecher Stowe's *Uncle Tom's Cabin* is known almost exclusively as an instrument of historical change, but Stowe's novel deserves critical respect for its convincing characters and their speech. — AES, v.10, no.2 (February 1967) 81. no.457.

"Manicheans," *Times Literary Supplement*, no.3340 (March 3, 1966) 153-4.

"Murder Most Fair by Agatha the Good, *Life*, v. 63 (December 1, 1967) 8.

"My Dear Students; a Letter," *New York Times Magazine*, November 19, 1972, p. 20
> Affectionately describes and condemns attitudes and scholarly failings of his New York City students.

"Moses in a Lounge Suit," *Spectator*, v. 224, no. 7395 (March 21, 1970) 374.
> Review of the *New English Bible*.

"The Novel in 2000 A.D.," *New York Times Book Review*, March 29, 1970, p. 2.

"The Novelist's Sources are Myth, Language, and the Here and Now," *New York Times Book Review*, July 19, 1964, p. 5.

"Our Bedfellow, the Marquis de Sade," *Horizon,* v.11 (Winter (1969) 104-9.

> De Sade distinguished himself as a cavalry officer during the Seven Year's War, 1756-1763. Arrested for debauchery in 1763, his life from then on was a matter of arrest, trial and imprisonment. He saw a world in which man's appetites for pleasure were best fulfilled through the exercise of power and cruelty. He was saved from the guillotine by the fall of Robespierre. De Sade's view of mankind as evil has been accepted in most of our literature. The author cites William Golding's *The Inheritors* as an example. — *Historical Abstracts.* A: Modern History, v.18, no.1 (Spring 1972) 70-71. no.18:747.

"Partridge in a Word Tree," *Encounter,* v. 33 (July 1969) 51-5.

"Politics of Graham Greene," *New York Times Book Review,* September 10, 1967, p.2.

"The Politics of Graham Greene." In *Page 2: The Best of "Speaking of Books" from the New York Times Book Review,* ed. by Francis Brown, p.284-91. New York: Holt, Rinehart and Winston, 1969.

"Portrait of the Artist in Middle Age," *Nation,* v.206 (March 4, 1968) 309-10.

"The Post-War American Novel; a View from the Periphery," *American Scholar,* v.35 (Winter 1965-66) 150-6.

"Powers that Be," *Encounter,* v.24, no.1 (January 1965) 71-76.

> Review article of C. P. Snow's *Corridors of Power* and Angus Wilson's *Late Call.* Though Wilson writes about power and responsibility with more authority than does Snow, both authors are "ornaments of the contemporary novel of the middle

way." — AES, v.9, no.1 (January 1966) 22. no.115.

"The Price of Gormenghast," *Spectator*, v. 224, no. 7408 (June 20, 1970) 819.
Review of *A World Away* by Maeve Gilmore.

"Private Dialect of Husbands and Wives," *Vogue*, v. 151 (June 1968) 118-9.

"The Professional Viewpoint," *Twentieth Century Studies*, v.1, no.2 (November 1969) 109-130.
Attitudes toward the treatment of sexual themes in the modern novel are expressed here by Anthony Burgess, Pamela Hansford Johnson, Jack Kerouac, John Updike, John Wain and others. — AES, v.13, no.8 (April 1970) 481.

"Pronounced Vla-DEEM-ear Nah-BOAK-off," *New York Times Book Review*, July 2, 1967, p.1, 20.
Review of Andrew Field's *Nabokov: His Life in Art*.

"Reading Your Own," *New York Times Book Review*, June 4, 1967, p.6.

"Said Mr. Cooper to his Wife: You Know, I Could Write Something Better Than That," *New York Times Magazine*, May 7, 1972, p.108.

"Seeing the Shape of Things to Come," *New York Times Book Review*, August 3, 1969, p.1.
Review of Lovat Dickson's *H. G. Wells*.

"Seen Any Good Galsworthy Lately?" *New York Times Magazine*, November 16, 1969, VI, p.57.
Article on Galsworthy's life and works, prompted by international success of TV series, based on his sequence of novels *The Forsyte Saga*.

"The Seventeenth Novel," *New York Times Book Review*, August 21, 1966, p.2.

"The Seventeenth Novel." In *Page 2: The Best of "Speaking of Books" from the New York Times Book Review*, ed. by Francis Brown, p. 85-89. New York: Holt, Rinehart and Winston, 1969.

"Silence, Exile and Cunning," *Listener*, v.73, no.1884 (May 6, 1965) 661-3.
> In Joyce's life and works there is a "strange fusion of the lowly and the exalted": the real world of pub tables and sawdust-covered floors and the metaphysical world of Catholicism. He searched for the cunning by which to "overcome the domination of . . . Mother Ireland . . . and Mother Church," and so became an exile. — AES, v.9, no.9 (November 1966) 576 no.2993.

"Singapore Revisited," *Spectator*, v.224, no.7406 (June 6, 1970) 742.

"Smooth Beawties," *Spectator*, v.224, no.7389 (February 7, 1970) 179-180.
> Review of *The Works of Thomas Campion*, ed. by Walter R. Davis.

"Speaking of Writing," *Times*, January 16, 1964, p.13.

"Steinerian Agony," *Encounter*, v.29 (December 1967) 79-82.

"Travel 18th Century Style," *Holiday*, v.42 (November 1967) 72-7.

"Treasures and Fetters," *Spectator, v. 212, no. 7078 (February 21, 1964) 254.*

> Review article of Elizabeth Bowen's *The Little Girls.* Elizabeth Bowen's true progenitor is Henry James. But where James articulates a whole culture, Miss Bowen conserves a particular place at a particular time. Her first novel in nine years shows that "atmosphere" is still her business. — AES, v.7, no.6 (June 1964) 304. no.1526.

"The Two Shaws," *Spectator, v.214, no.7141 (May 7, 1965) 635-6.*

> Review article of *The Complete Plays of Bernard Shaw; The Complete Prefaces of Bernard Shaw.* What makes Shaw great as a dramatist ("perhaps second only to Shakespeare") is the sudden thrust of the prophetic, a sense of the numinous, coupled with a dramaturgical instinct so powerful that it threatened to rob him of his identity. So Shaw, "anxious to be the known, feared and respected teacher," wrote his prefaces to show the world the "finger-pointing, beard-wagging" figure called GBS. — AES, v.9, no.3 (March 1966) 193. no.1012.

"Vieux Chapeau," *New York Times Book Review,* March 3, 1968, p.4-5.

> Review of Simone de Beauvoir's *Les Belles Images.*

"Viewpoint," *Times Literary Supplement,* April 21, 1972, p.446.

"What is Pornography?" In *Perspectives on Pornography,* ed. by Douglas A. Hughes, p.4-8. New York: St. Martin's Press, 1970.

"What Now in the Novel?" *Spectator, v.214, no.7135 (March 26, 1965) 400.*

> There is evidence that the "junior novelists" are dissatisfied with the subject matter inherited from the Fifties and are more

interested in form than content. — AES, v.9, no.3 (March 1966) 193. no.1010.

"What's All This Fuss About Libraries?" *Library Journal,* v.93 (March 15, 1968) 1114-15.

"Woman and Women," *Vogue,* v.154 (October 1, 1969) 194.

"Words," In *The English Language,* ed. by Whitney French Bolton and David Crystal, v.2, p.294-304. London: Cambridge University Press, 1969.

"Work and Play," *New York Times Book Review,* June 5, 1966, p.1.

"The Writer and Music," *The Listener,* v.57 (May 3, 1962) 761-62.

"The Writer as Drunk," *Spectator,* v.217, no.7219 (November 4, 1966) 588.
> Review article of Rae Jeff's *Brendan Behan; Man and Showman.* Both pub-men, Dylan Thomas and Behan were rhetorical writers with "an ancestral memory of the word-man's social function, the bardic job." For them, pub-drinking remained the last of our creative social acts. — AES, v.10, no.8 (October 1967) 538. no.2890.

"The Writer's Purpose," *New York Times Book Review,* May 1, 1966, p.2.

Books and Dissertations

Brown, Rexford Glenn. *Conflict and Confluence: the Art of Anthony Burgess.*
    Unpublished Ph.D. dissertation — University of Iowa. *Dissertations Abstracts International* no.5220-A.

De Vitis, A. A. *Anthony Burgess.* New York: Twayne Publishers, 1972.

Dix, Carl M. *Anthony Burgess.* Edited by Ian Scott-Kilvert. London: Longman, 1971.

Morris, Robert K. *The Consolations of Ambiguity; an Essay on the Novels of Anthony Burgess.* Columbia: University of Missouri Press, 1971.

Stinson, John Jerome. *The Uses of the Grotesque and Other Modes of Distortion: Philosophy and Implication in the Novels of Iris Murdoch, William Golding, Anthony Burgess, and J. P. Donleavy.*
    Unpublished Ph.D. dissertation — New York University. *Dissertation Abstracts International* no.1533-A.

Periodical Articles, Essays, Etc.

Adler, Dick. "Inside Mr. Burgess," *Sunday Time Magazine*, April 2, 1967, p.47-50.

Aggeler, Geoffrey. "The Comic Art of Anthony Burgess," *Arizona Quarterly*, v.25, no.3 (Autumn 1969) 234-51.

Aggeler, Geoffrey. "Mr. Enderby and Mr. Burgess," *Malahat Review*, v.10 (April 1969) 104-110.

"Anthony Burgess; the Author of *A Clockwork Orange* Now Switches His Attention to Napoleon's Stomach," *Publishers' Weekly*, v.201 (January 31, 1972) 182-3.

Bergonzi, Bernard. *The Situation of the Novel.* London: Macmillan, 1970.
    Burgess passim.

Betts, Ernest. "Millions on a Musical about Shakespeare," *London Times*, August 24, 1968, p.18.

Brooke-Rose, Christine. "Le Roman Experimental en Angleterre," *Les Langues Moderne*, v.63, no.2 (March-April 1969) 158.

"Burgess, Anthony," *Contemporary Authors; a bio-bibliographical guide to current authors and their works.* Detroit: Gale Research, 1962-   . See v.1-4, p.136-7.

"Burgess, Anthony," *Current Biography*, v.33, no.5 (May 1972) 11-13.

"Burgess, Anthony," *Current Biography Yearbook 1972*, p.54-57. New York: Wilson, 1973.

"Burgess, Anthony," *National Observer*, April 27, 1970, p.19.

"Burgess, Anthony," *200 Contemporary Authors*, edited by Barbara Harte and Carolyn Riley, p.60. Detroit: Gale Research, 1969.

"Burgess, Anthony," *Who's Who*, 1970-71.

"Burgess, Anthony," *Who's Who*, World, 1971.

"Burgess, Anthony," In "Literature of the Early Sixties," *Wilson Library Bulletin*, v.39, no.9 (May 1965) 748.77.
>An omnibus review of many different authors. The short section on Burgess briefly praises his novel *Honey for the Bears*.

Chew, Shirley. "Mr. Livedog's Day," *Encounter*, v.38, no.6 (June 1972) 57-64.

Clemons, Walter. "Anthony Burgess: Pushing On," *New York Times Book Review*. November 29, 1970, p.2.
>A short biographical sketch of Burgess' life.

Dahlie, Hallvard. "Brian Moore: An Interview,"*Tamarack Review*, no. 46 (Winter 1968) 7-29.
>Moore finds American fiction "more ambitious" than English fiction at the present moment, and he considers Bellow, the best living American novelist, a superior craftsman to English novelist Burgess. Of his own work, Moore points out

that the basic theme in his novels centers in the gap he per-
ceives "between the different selves we are at different times
of our life." — AES, v.11, no.10 (December 1968) 552.

Davis, Earle. "Laugh Now — Think Later! The Genius of Anthony Burgess," *Kansas Magazine* (Manhat-
tan, Kansas) 1968, p.7-12.

Engelborghs, Maurits. "Romans van een Woordkun-
stenaar," (Novels by an Artist in Words), Dietsche
Warande en Belfort (Antwerp) no.1, p.59-62.

Hicks, J. "Eclectic Author of His Own Five Foot
Shelf," *Life,* v.65 (October 25, 1968) 87+.

Hicks, Granville. "Fertile World of Anthony Burgess," *Saturday Review,* v.50 (July 15, 1967) 27+.

Hoffmann, Charles G. and A. C. "Mr. Kell and Mr.
Burgess: Inside and Outside Mr. Enderby." In *The
Shaken Realist: Essays in Modern Literature in Hon-
or of Frederick J. Hoffman,* ed. by Melvin J. Fried-
man and John B. Vickery. p.300-10. Baton Rouge:
Louisiana State University Press, 1970.

Horder, John. "Art That Pays," *Guardian,* October
10, 1964, p.5.

Hyman, S. F. "Anthony Burgess." In *On Contemporary Literature; an Anthology of Critical Essays on the
Major Movements and Writers of Contemporary Literature,* ed. by Richard Kostelanetz, p.300-305.
New York: Avon, 1964.

Isnard, Marcel. "Anthony Burgess," *Etudes
Anglaises,* v.19, no.1 (January/March 1966) 45-54.

Kermode, Frank. "Poetry and Borborygms," *Listener,* v.79 (June 6, 1968) 735-6.

LeClair, T. "Essential Opposition: The Novels of Anthony Burgess," *Critique,* v.12, no.3 (1971) 77-94.

Mitchell, James Alexander Hugh. *The God I Want.* London: Constable, 1967.
This book chronicles "personal attempts by individual writers and thinkers to forget all they have ever learned about the Christian God or other gods and to ask themselves what god, if any, they really want." Anthony Burgess is one of the top contributors.

Mitchell, Julian. "Anthony Burgess," *London Magazine,* v.3, no.11 (February 1964) 48-54.
In all of Anthony Burgess' novels, 12 published since 1956, the 'hero' is Pelagian by instinct and harried by Augustinian doubts. Thus capable of suffering endless humiliations, his only satisfaction is to accept the world as it throws itself at him. Burgess' way of presenting and varying this predicament is remarkable. Endowed with a rich imagination, and teeming with ideas, he uses all the novelist's tricks to obtain the density and complexity he wants. — AES, v.7, no.6 (June 1964) 284. no.1412.

Nichols, Lewis. "Mr. Burgess," *New York Times Book Review,* April 10, 1966, p.8.

Nordell, Rod. "Fiction: The Comedy of Discontent," *Christian Science Monitor,* v.53, no.46 (January 19, 1961) 5.
Many young writers, like Wilfred Sheed in *A Middle Class Education,* Anthony Burgess in *The Right to an Answer,* and Terry Southern in *The Magic Christian,* use the comic novel to express social and moral discontent. These "budding novelists" use characters without morals to ridicule the barrenness of modern civilization. "They thrust their moral confusion at

the reader, challenging him to offer something better." — AES, v.4, no.4 (April 1961) 151-2. no.725.

Page, Malcolm. "Anthony Burgess: The Artist as Performer," *West Coast Review*, v.4, no.3 (January 1970) 21-4.

Burgess, who visited Simon Fraser University on March 5, 1969, seemed to be an unhappy lapsed Catholic who covered his near despair for himself and society with mingled humor and cynicism. He is a man of restless imagination, full of provocative generalizations about contemporary writers, patient with television and newspaper interviewers, and he revealed himself as the veteran schoolteacher in a lecture to 350 university people.—AES, v.14, no.8 (April 1971) 517, no.2447.

Pritchard, W. H. "Novels of Anthony Burgess," *Massachusetts Review*, v.7, no.3 (Summer 1966) 525-39.

Burgess's early novels are comic; and like those of Dickens', verbal and theatrical. After 1962 his works are concerned with the individual and the modern state; they are fantasies or fables which appeal to us in odd and disturbing ways. His experimentation in recent works has caused the unjustified criticism that he has overreached himself. — AES, v.12, no.5 (May 1969) 248.

Riemer, G. "Interview," *National Elementary Principal*, v.50, no.6 (May 1971) 9-21.

Solotaroff, Theodore. "The Busy Hand of Burgess," In *The Red Hot Vacuum, and Other Pieces on the Writing of the Sixties*, p.269-75. New York: Atheneum, 1970.

Sullivan, Walter. "Death Without Tears: Anthony Burgess and the Dissolution of the West," *Hollins Critic*, v.6, no.2 (April 1969) 1-11.

Wood, Michael. "A Dream of Clockwork Oranges," *New Society*, June 6, 1968, p.842-3.

Reviews

Age of the Grand Tour
Library Journal, v.93 (January 1, 1968) 77.
Nation, v.205 (December 25, 1967) 697.
New York Times Book Review, December 3, 1967, p.62.
New Yorker, v.43 (December 9, 1967) 246.
Times Literary Supplement, February 8, 1968, p.135.

Beds in the East
New Statesman, v.57, no.1469 (May 9, 1959) 663.
(See also reviews ot the trilogy, *The Long Day Wanes,* of which this book is a part).

Coaching Days of England
Book Week, December 11, 1966, p.5.
Library Journal, v.92 (February 15, 1967) 765.
New York Review of Books, v.8 (May 18, 1967) 13.
New York Times Book Review, December 4, 1966, p.42.
Saturday Review, v.49 (December 3, 1966) 33.

Clockwork Orange (Book)
Hudson Review, v.16, no.2 (Summer 1963) 281-89.
Kenyon Review, v.25, no.3 (Summer 1963) 559.
Library Journal, v.88 (February 15, 1963) 793.
New Leader, v.46, no.1 (January 7, 1963) 22.
New Statesman, v.63 (May 18, 1962) 718.
New York Herald Tribune Book Review, April 14, 1963, p.7.
New York Times Book Review, April 7, 1963, p.36.
People's World, San Francisco, Calif., June 22, 1963, p.5.
Show, August 1963, p.38-40.
Time, v.81 (February 15, 1963) 103.
Times Literary Supplement, May 25, 1962, p.377.

Clockwork Orange (Film)
American Scholar, v.4 (Summer 1972) 439-43.

Atlantic, v.229 (March 1972) 100-4.
Christian Century, v.89 (February 15, 1972) 207.
Christian Century, v.89 (September 6, 1972) 878.
Commentary, v.53 (March 1972) 79-82.
Commonweal, v.95 (January 14, 1972) 351-2.
Commonweal, v.96 (July 14, 1972) 383-6.
Film Heritage, v.7, no.4 (Summer 1972) 1-6.
Film Heritage, v.7, no.4 (Summer 1972) 7-18.
Film Quarterly, v.25 (Spring 1972) 33-6.
Life, v.72 (February 4, 1972) 14.
Nation, v.214 (January 3, 1972) 28.
New Republic, v.166 (January 1, 1972) 22.
New York Review of Books, v.18, no.6 (April 6, 1972) 28-31.
New Yorker, v.47 (January 1, 1972) 50-3.
Newsweek, v.79 (January 3, 1972) 28-33.
Saturday Review, v.54 (December 25, 1971) 40-1.
Time, 98 (December 20, 1971) 80-1.
Time, 98 (December 27, 1971) 59.

Cyrano de Bergerac

Atlantic, v.229 (January 1972) 97.
New York Times Book Review, December 26, 1971, p.6.

Devil of a State

Guardian, November 10, 1961, p.6.
Kirkus, v.29 (November 1, 1961) 979.
Listener, v.66 (December 28, 1961) 1133.
New Statesman, v.62 (November 24, 1961) 802.
New York Herald Tribune Review of Books, March 4, 1962, p.13.
New York Times Book Review, February 25, 1962, p.40.
Punch, v.241, no.6323 (November 15, 1961) 731.
Saturday Review, v.45 (March 17, 1962) 27.
Spectator, v.207, no.6958 (November 3, 1961) p.636.
Springfield Republican, March 11, 1962, Sect. D, p.4.
Times Literary Supplement, November 17, 1961, p.829.

Doctor is Sick

America, v.114 (April 30, 1966) 630.

Book Week, May 15, 1966, p.14.

Choice, v.3 (July 1966) 407.

Commonweal, v.84 (May 20, 1966) 260.

Critic, v.25 (October 1966) 114.

Library Journal, v.91 (April 1, 1966) 1920.

New York Review of Books, v.6 (June 9, 1966) 20.

New York Times Book Review, April 24, 1966, p.5.

Punch, v.239, no.6275 (December 21, 1960) 909.

Saturday Review, v.49 (May 7, 1966) 95.

Southern Review, N.S., v.3, no.4 (Autumn 1967) 1050-1061.

Spectator, v.205, no.6909 (November 25, 1960) 860.

Time, v.87 (April 29, 1966) 114.

Time and Tide, v.41, no.48 (November 26, 1960) 1445.

Enderby

Best Sellers, v.28 (June 15, 1968) 126.

Book World, June 9, 1968, p.13.

Choice, v.5 (July 1968) 620.

Commonweal, v.80 (November 15, 1968) 262.

Contemporary Literature, v.11, no.3 (Summer 1970) 401.

Critic, v.27 (October 1968) 95.

Encounter, v.31, no.4 (October 1968) 74.

Hudson Review, v.21, no.4 (Winter 1968-69) 764.

Library Journal, v.93 (June 1, 1968) 2257.

Listener, v.79, no.2045 (June 6, 1968) 735.

Masterplots Annual, 1969, p.115.

Nation, v.207 (July 22, 1968) 58.

National Review, v.20 (June 18, 1968) 613.

New Leader, v.51 (September 9, 1968) 20.

New Republic, v.159 (August 24, 1968) 20.

New York Review of Books, v.11 (August 22, 1968) 34.

New York Times Book Review, June 30, 1968, p.5.

New Yorker, v.44 (June 29, 1968) 87.

Saturday Review, v.51 (June 8, 1968) 37.

Spectator, v.220 no.7301 (May 31, 1968) 745.

Tablet, May 25, 1968, p.529.

Time, v.91 (June 14, 1968) 93.

Enderby Outside. SEE Enderby.

Eve of Saint Venus.

America, v.122 (May 23, 1970) 565.
Best Sellers, v.30 (May 15, 1970) 67.
Book World, April 19, 1970, p.3.
Choice, v.7 (November, 1970) 1229.
Library Journal, v.95 (June 1, 1970) 2179.
Listener, v.72, no.1850 (September 10, 1964) 401.
New Leader, v.53, no.11 (May 25, 1970) 22-24.
New Republic, v.162 (May 9, 1970) 43.
Saturday Review, v.53 (May 16, 1970) 48.
Spectator, v.213, no.7107 (September 11, 1964) 346.
Time, v.95 (April 27, 1970) 96.

Here Comes Everybody. SEE *Re Joyce.*

Honey for the Bears.

America, v.110 (February 8, 1964) 200.
Antioch Review, v.24, no.3 (Fall 1964) 408.
Book Week, February 9, 1964, p.6.
Library Journal, v.89 (February 1, 1964) 651.
Listener, v.69, no.1774 (March 28, 1963) 567.
New Leader, v.47, no.8 (April 13, 1964) 22.
New Statesman, v.65 (April 5, 1963) 496.
New York Herald Tribune Book Review, February 9, 1964, p.6.
New York Review of Books, v.1 (January 23, 1964) 7.
New York Times Book Review, February 2, 1964, p.5.
Newsweek, v.63 (February 3, 1964) 81.
Punch, v.244, no.6395 (April 3, 1963) 498.
Saturday Review, v.47 (February 29, 1964) 81.
Southern Review, N.S., v.5, no.1 (January 1969) 259.
Spectator, v.210, no.7034 (April 19, 1963) 504.
Time, v.83 (January 24, 1964) 70.
Times Literary Supplement, March 29, 1963, p.213.

Inside Mr. Enderby. SEE *Enderby.*

Journal of the Plague Year

Times Literary Supplement, no.3370, September 29, 1966,
p.901.

Language Made Plain

Christian Science Monitor, March 1, 1965, p.13.
Library Journal, v.90 (June 1, 1965) 2554.
New York Times Book Review, March 28, 1965, p.26.
Times Literary Supplement, April 23, 1964, p.337.
Modern Language Review, v.60, no.1 (January 1965) 84.

The Long Day Wanes

Best Sellers, v.25, (July 1, 1965) 150.
Hudson Review, v.18, no.3 (Autumn 1965) 449.
New Leader, v.48, no.10 (May 10, 1965) 24-25.
New York Review of Books, v.4 (May 20, 1965) 15.
New York Times Book Review, May 30, 1965, p.14.
Pacific Affairs, v.38, no.2 (Summer 1965) 206.
Time, v.86 (July 2, 1965) 84.

Malayan Trilogy. SEE The Long Day Wanes.

MF

America, v.124 (June 12, 1971) 616.
Atlantic, v.227 (May 1971) 114.
Best Sellers, v.31 (April 1, 1971) 15.
Book World, March 21, 1971, p.3.
Commonweal, v.94 (May 28, 1971) 290.
Library Journal, v.96 (March 15, 1971) 976.
Listener, v.85, no.2203 (June 17, 1971) 790.
New Statesman, v.81 (June 16, 1971) 856.
New York Times Book Review, April 4, 1971, p.4.
Newsweek, v.77 (April 19, 1971) 120.
Saturday Review, v.54 (March 27, 1971) 31.
Time, v.97 (March 22, 1971) 80.
Times Literary Supplement, June 18, 1971, p.693.

Nothing Like the Sun

Best Sellers, v.24 (October 1, 1964) 259.
Book Week, September 20, 1964, p.5
Commonweal, v.81 (October 30, 1964) 174.
Hudson Review, v.17, no.4 (Winter, 1964/65) 608.
Listener, v.71, no.1830 (April 23, 1964) 693.

Masterplots Annual, 1965, p.215.

Nation, v.199 (October 5, 1964) 196.

New Statesman, v.67 (April 24, 1964) 642.

New York Herald Tribune Book Review, September 20, 1964, p.5.

New York Times Book Review, September 13, 1964, p.5.

Saturday Review, v.47 (October 17, 1964) 38.

Show, v.4, no.11 (December 1964) 80.

Southern Review, N.S., v.2, no.4 (October 1966) 952.

Spectator, v.212, no.7087 (April 24, 1964) 561.

Times Literary Supplement, April 23, 1964, p.329.

Novel Now; A Guide to Contemporary Fiction

Book World, December 3, 1967, p.32.

Hudson Review, v.21, no.2 (Summer 1968) 355.

Library Journal, v.92 (October 15, 1967) 3642.

Massachusetts Review (Winter 1968) 181.

New York Times Book Review, January 7, 1968, p.18.

Saturday Review, v.50 (November 25, 1967) 33.

Sewanee Review, v.77, no.1 (January-March 1969) 164.

Spectator, v.219, no.7260 (August 18, 1967) 190.

One Hand Clapping

Best Sellers, v.31 (February 15, 1972) 514.

Book World, March 5, 1972, p.7.

Christian Science Monitor, February 10, 1972, p.10.

Library Journal, v.97 (February 15, 1972) 698.

New York Times Book Review, March 12, 1972, p.4.

New Yorker, v.48 (March 18, 1972) 154.

Newsweek, v.79 (March 6, 1972) 78.

Saturday Review, v.55 (February 12, 1972) 73.

Time, v.99 (February 14, 1972) 73.

Re Joyce

Carleton Miscellany, v.7, no.2 (Spring 1966) 124.

Choice, v.3 (July 1966) 408.

Commonweal, v.83 (March 4, 1966) 645.

Criticism, v.9, no.1 (Winter 1967) 102.

Dublin Magazine, v.5, no.1 (Spring 1966) 85.

Economist, v.217 (December 4, 1965) 1095.

Encounter, v.25 (November 1965) 78-82.

English, v.16, no.93 (Autumn 1966) 111.

Harper, v.232 (March 1966) 142.

James Joyce Quarterly, v.3, no.3 (Spring 1966) 215-219.

Listener, v.74, no.1911 (November 11, 1965) 767.

Modern Language Review, v.62, no.4 (October 1967) 714.

New Statesman, v.70 (September 17, 1965) 402.

New York Times Book Review, January 9, 1966, p.6.

New Yorker, v.41 (January 15, 1966) 120.

Saturday Review, v.48 (December 25, 1965) 34.

Southern Review, N.S., v.4, no.1 (January 1968) 259.

Spectator, v.215, no.7161 (September 24, 1965) 384.

Tablet, November 6, 1965, p.1241.

Times Literary Supplement, November 4, 1965, p.972.

Right to An Answer

Booklist, v.57 (January 15, 1961) 292.

Chicago Sunday Tribune, January 8, 1961, p.4.

Christian Science Monitor, January 19, 1961, p.5.

Guardian, May 27, 1960, p.9.

Kirkus, v.28 (November 1, 1960) 937.

Library Journal, v.85 (December 15, 1960) 4485.

Listener, v.63, no.1630 (June 23, 1960) 1111

New York Herald Tribune Lively Arts, January 22, 1961, p.32.

New Yorker, v.37 (April 8, 1961) 169.

Punch, v.238, no.6244 (May 25, 1960) 739.

Saturday Review, v.44 (January 28, 1961) 17.

Spectator, v.204, no.6883 (May 27, 1960) 778.

Springfield Republican, January 29, 1961, Sec. D, p.4.

Time, v.77 (January 20, 1961) 91.

Time and Tide, v.41, no.24 (June 11, 1960) 679.

Times Literary Supplement, June 3, 1960, p.349.

Shakespeare

Atlantic, v.226 (November 1970) 143.

Best Sellers, v.30 (November 15, 1970) 357.

Commonweal, v.93 (October 30, 1970) 131.

Economist, v.237 (October 17, 1970) 60.

Library Journal, v.95 (November 15, 1970) 3909.

New Statesman, v.80 (December 25, 1970) 870.
Saturday Review, v.53 (November 7, 1970) 46.
Times Literary Supplement, December 11, 1970, p.1440.

A Shorter Finnegan's Wake
Book Week, February 19, 1967, p.12.
Choice, v.4 (June 1967) 422.
Dublin Magazine, v.6, no.1 (Spring 1967) 94.
James Joyce Quarterly, v.4, no.2 (Winter 1967) 137-139.
Library Journal, v.92 (January 1, 1967) 134.
New York Times Book Review, October 1, 1967, p.38.
Spectator, v.216, no.7200 (June 24, 1966) 794.
Time, v.89 (February 24, 1967) 92.

Tremor of Intent
America, v.115 (October 22, 1966) 492.
Best Sellers, v.26 (October 15, 1966) 254.
Book Week, October 9, 1966, p.2.
Commonweal, v.85 (December 16, 1966) 2.
Hudson Review, v.19, no.4 (Winter 1966/67) 659.
Library Journal, v.91 (November 1, 1966) 5426.
Listener, v.75, no.1941 (June 9, 1966) 849.
Nation, v.203 (December 5, 1966) 620.
New Republic, v.155 (October 15, 1966) 25.
New Statesman, v.71 (June 10, 1966) 852.
New York Times Book Review, October 16, 1966, p.4.
Partisan Review, v.34, no.2 (Spring 1967) 319.
Saturday Review, v.49 (October 29, 1966) 32.
Southern Review, N.S., v.5, no.1 (January 1969) 224.
Spectator, v.216, no.7198 (June 10, 1966) 733.
Tablet, July 30, 1966, p.872.
Time, v.88 (October 14, 1966) 125.
Times Literary Supplement, June 9, 1966, p.509.

Urgent Copy
America, v.120 (March 29, 1969) 369.
Best Sellers, v.29 (April 1, 1969) 3.
Catholic World, July 1969, p.190.
Library Journal, v.94 (March 15, 1969) 1147.

Listener, v.80, no.2067 (November 7, 1968) 618.
London Magazine, v.8, no.8 (November 1968) 110-112.
New Statesman, v.76 (November 15, 1968) 678.
New York Times Book Review, March 30, 1969, p.4.
Progressive, v.33, no.5 (May 1969) 48.
Queen's Quarterly, v.76, no.2 (Summer 1969) 366.
Time, v.93 (April 11, 1969) 108.
Times Literary Supplement, March 13, 1969, p.259.

Vision of Battlements

Choice, v.3 (July 1966) 408.
Commonweal, v.84 (March 25, 1966) 33.
English Studies, v.47, no.4 (August 1966) 316.
Library Journal, v.91 (April 1, 1966) 1920.
Listener, v.74, no.1905 (September 30, 1965) 505.
New Statesman, v.70 (September 24, 1965) 444.
New York Times Book Review, January 30, 1966, p.32.
New Yorker, v.42 (May 7, 1966) 186.
Newsweek, v.67 (February 21, 1966) 103.
Saturday Review, v.49 (January 29, 1966) 38.
Southern Review, v.3, no.2 (April 1967) 444.
Spectator, v.215, no.7162 (October 1, 1965) 424.
Time, v.87 (February 4, 1966) 107.
Times Literary Supplement, September 30, 1965, p.850.

The Wanting Seed

Best Sellers, v.23 (November 1, 1963) 277.
Book of the Month Club News, November 1963, p.13.
Book Week, November 3, 1963, p.6.
Commonweal, v.79 (January 17, 1964) 465.
Herald Tribune Book Week Magazine, October 29, 1963, p.23
Herald Tribune Book Week Magazine, November 3, 1963, p.6.
Library Journal, v.88 (October 1, 1963) 3641.
New Statesman, v.64 (October 5, 1962) 460.
New York Times Book Review, October 27, 1963, p.4.
New Yorker, v.39 (November 2, 1963) 209.
Newsweek, v.62 (October 28, 1963) 101.

Punch, v.243, no.6371 (October 17, 1962) 575.
Saturday Review, v.46 (November 23, 1963) 43.
Time, v.82 (December 6, 1963) 123.
Times Literary Supplement, October 5, 1962, p.773.

The Worm and the Ring
Punch, v.240, no.6302 (June 28, 1961) 989.
Spectator, v.206, no.6936 (June 2, 1961) 808.
Times Literary Supplement, July 7, 1961, p.421.

ANTHONY BURGESS
A CHRONOLOGICAL TABLE

1918   Born February 25, 1917, in Manchester. Son of Joseph Wilson, a pianist, and "Beautiful Belle Burgess," a musical comedy actress.

1918   Mother and only sister killed in influenza epidemic.

1940   Graduated from Manchester University with a B.A. degree in English literature.

Joined the British Army Education Corps. Served as musical director of a Special Services Unit. Became a Sergeant-Major. Left the army in 1946.

1942   Married Llewella Isherwood Jones. Wife attacked and assaulted by American deserters. The assault killed their unborn child. It contributed to her death in 1968.

1946- Lectured at Birmingham University. Employed
1948   by Armed Forces Central Advisory Council.

1948   Lecturer in phonetics for the Ministry of Education. Wrote *Vision of Battlements* (published 1965).

1950   Appointed English master at a grammar school in Banbury, near Oxford.

1954   Wrote *The Worm and the Ring* (published 1961).

1954- Served as an education officer for the Colonial
1959   Service in Malaya and Brunei, Borneo. In the East wrote the three novels which constitute the *Malayan Trilogy* (British title) or *The Long Day Wanes* (American title): *Time for a Tiger, Enemy in the Blanket* and *Beds in the East.*

1956   *Time for a Tiger.*

1958   *English Literature; A Survey for Students.*
       Enemy in the Blanket.

1959   Suffered headaches. Doctor diagnosed brain tumor. Returned to England and devoted his whole time to writing novels.

1959- Wrote *The Right to an Answer, The Doctor is*
1969   *Sick, The Wanting Seed, One hand Clapping* and *Inside Mr. Enderby*. The pseudonym Joseph Kell graced the last two titles. No trace of brain tumor.

1959   *Beds in the East.*

1960   *Doctor is Sick.*
       The Right to an Answer.

1961   *Devil of a State.*
       One Hand Clapping.
       The Worm and the Ring.

1962   *A Clockwork Orange.*
       The Wanting Seed.

1963   *Honey for the Bears.*
       Inside Mr. Enderby
       Novel Today.

1964   *Even of Saint Venus.*
       Language Made Plain.
       Malayan Trilogy.
       Nothing Like the Sun.
       Re Joyce.

1965   *Here Comes Everybody.*
       The Long Day Wanes. Includes *Time for a Tiger, Enemy in the Blanket* and *Beds in the East.*
       Vision of Battlements.

1966   *Coaching Days of England.*
       Tremor of Intent.

1967   *Age of the Grand Tour.*
       Novel Now.

1968   Llewella Jones, his first wife, died. Married Liliana Macellari, a teacher of linguistics at Cambridge.

       Exiled himself to Malta in October to escape confiscatory Welfare State Taxation. Remained briefly in Malta.

       Enderby Outside.
       Enderby. Includes *Inside Mr. Enderby* and *Enderby Outside.*
       Urgent Copy.

1969- Writer-in-residence at the University of North
1970 Carolina.

1970 *Shakespeare.*

1970- Taught writing at Princeton University; simul-
1971 taneously lectured at Columbia University.

1971 *MF.*
      Cyrano de Bergerac performed at the 1971 Sum-
      mer Festival of the Tyrone Guthrie Theatre in
      Minneapolis. Burgess translated and adapted the
      Rostand work and composed the music.

1972 Signed a three year contract with the Tyrone
      Guthrie Theatre, where he will serve as play-
      wright-in-residence.

1972- Spent a year as Distinguished Professor of Eng-
1973 lish at City College in New York.